Home Design Gardening

CREATE SMOOTH LINES LANDSCAPES USING STUNNING FLOWERS COMBINATIONS, EDIBLE HEDGES, AND BUILD PLEASANT WALKWAYS. SHAPE YOUR GARDEN TO BECOME A COLORFUL PAINTING

Mathews Holmes - Roger Markham

Copyright 2020 - All rights reserved.

The content contained within this book may not be reproduced, duplicated or transmitted without direct written permission from the author or the publisher.

Under no circumstances will any blame or legal responsibility be held against the publisher, or author, for any damages, reparation, or monetary loss due to the information contained within this book. Either directly or indirectly.

Legal Notice:

This book is copyright protected. This book is only for personal use. You cannot amend, distribute, sell, use, quote or paraphrase any part, or the content within this book, without the consent of the author or publisher.

Disclaimer Notice:

Please note the information contained within this document is for educational and entertainment purposes only. All effort has been executed to present accurate, up to date, and reliable, complete information. No warranties of any kind are declared or implied.
Readers acknowledge that the author is not engaging in the rendering of legal, financial, medical or professional advice. The content within this book has been derived from various sources. Please consult a licensed professional before attempting any techniques outlined in this book.

By reading this document, the reader agrees that under no circumstances is the author responsible for any losses, direct or indirect, which are incurred as a result of the use of information contained within this document, including, but not limited to, - errors, omissions, or inaccuracies.

Table of Contents

INTRODUCTION — 5

CHAPTER 1
What is Landscape Gardening? — 9

CHAPTER 2
Paint Your Picture with Plants — 15

CHAPTER 3
Landscape Care: Fertilizers, Weeds, Watering — 29

CHAPTER 4
How to Enhance Your Garden with Pots, Containers, Raised Bed? — 39

CHAPTER 5
How to Build A to Give MoreCharm to Your Garden? — 45

CHAPTER 6
Different Examples of Landscapes — 55

CHAPTER 7
A Patio Garden Provide Privacy and Pleasure Like an Outdoor Living Room — 63

CHAPTER 8
Garden Geometry Transform A Small Front Yard — 71

CHAPTER 9
What Are the Essential Tools That You Need? — 75

CHAPTER 10
Irrigation System — 83

CHAPTER 11
Designing Landscape Garden — 91

CHAPTER 12
Rules of (Green) Thumb for Garden Design — 97

CHAPTER 13
Design with Family in Mind — 103

CHAPTER 14
Containers Bed Borders for Plants Ideas — 109

CHAPTER 15
Designing with Evergreens — 119

CONCLUSION — 125

INTRODUCTION

Do you want a formal or an informal landscape?

Before you start to design your landscape, you're going to make a list of everything you'd like to have in your landscape. A pool? Fence? An entertainment area? A deck? A pergola? An outdoor kitchen? An outdoor fireplace? Lots of flowers? Trees?

Write down everything you'd like to have in your landscape.

Keep your lifestyle in mind.

If you have kids, they need a place to play. The same with pets. They'll need a grass area to play and do their business.

If you have kids and pets, a large flower bed in the middle of your yard probably won't work. Kids will run across the yard and the last thing on their minds is avoiding a flower bed. Use the sides of your yard for flowers and plants. Or create flower beds around trees.

- Before you start drawing your new landscape design, take some time to sit in your yard. Take your sketch and go outside early in the morning, at noon, and early evening.

Make notes on your sketch of areas that get full sun, shade, partial shade, views, breezes, and problem areas.

If you have plants or anything else you want to remove, consider relocating them instead of discarding them. Maybe relocate shrubs or trees blocking a summer breeze to an area you want to block neighbors. Write notes on your design of all the items you want to remove or relocate.

Take advantage of views. In the sample sketch, you'll see there is a view to a park. What could you do in this area? Maybe a sitting area. An arbor will add height. Plant vines on either side of the arbor that will climb the trellis and add more color to your yard. Maybe a table and chairs, a wooden bench, a "natural" bench made from large stones. Use your imagination.

Write down all problem areas on your sketch and find solutions.

You'll notice in the sample sketch there is a low wet area. It's a problem area.

One solution would be to build up the land using soil and rocks, or maybe a dry creek bed with large rocks and plants, or dig a ditch and install a drain pipe to relocate water to another area of your yard.

I've seen many landscapes not conducive to homeowners' lifestyles. A family with kids and pets designs a formal landscape. They don't enjoy their landscape because they're afraid it will get damaged - limiting the areas where kids can play and keeping the dogs in a pen. Looking at a formal garden from your window is nice but what fun is it if you're constantly worrying about the dog digging up plants or the kids running through your flower beds?

Do you enjoy watching the sunrise and sunset?

Plan a sitting area with a view facing east and west.

Would you rather spend the weekends doing something other than yard work?

Include elements that require minimal or no maintenance.

Are you concerned about conserving water?

Select drought-tolerant plants.

Make a list of everything you'd like to have in your landscape. Keeping your lifestyle in mind will provide you with an outdoor area you will use and enjoy.

CHAPTER 1
What is Landscape Gardening?

Our usual concern is to improve our yards or business establishments because all of us value beauty. We put flowering plants in different places, fences that serve as barriers, table and chairs to have outdoor refreshment or meal, swings, garden gnomes, and other material items that we want to have in our lawns. These and other activities that suppose a particular area to be developed are collectively called landscaping. Most landowners prefer a landscape garden. What is gardening in the landscape? As its name suggests, it is a kind of landscape which transforms an area into a garden.

Gardening is essentially a process design making use of living elements, especially plants, both flowering and non-flowering plants. Garden owners can do this, but others are hiring professional landscapers to develop their gardens. The basic principles of gardening have been trained by professional landscapers, and others may take short courses for that. On the other hand, when spending time working at their own gardens, garden owners obtain good experiences. Other people have made this a hobby, especially women, while others make it as an expansion of their creativity. But whoever does the planting, whether it's a traditional housewife or a professional landscaper, understanding what landscape gardening is all about can result in the successful creation of a garden that meets the landowner's aim, needs or desires. The gardening, meanwhile, is not just about the designs and templates. It is also about how it would be maintained after it has been put up after all the dynamic landscape gardening is. Acting with it continues as long as there are tendentious plants and flowers and buildings to maintain. You can add or remove buildings, you can renovate them, you can grow other flowers or trees, or you can do something to enhance your garden continually.

What's nice about landscaping is that you can do your own style your way around it. There is no limit to it, and there are no defined rules on what can only be done to your garden. As long as you know what landscape gardening is and its fundamental principles, then you're ready to begin. Or if you don't feel confident enough, you can hire professional landscapers to make the garden you want. The services may be expensive but rest assured that it can be of great benefit to you.

Landscaping for Privacy

If you've ever set out to build your property with a privacy fence, you know what an expensive hassle it can be. You will dig holes which are two feet deep, mix and pour together concrete, and nail countless boards. All has to be level, in a straight line. It will cost several thousand dollars to pay somebody to do this. There is, however, a more straightforward way of producing the same results by innovative landscaping.

When they're brand new, privacy fences may be attractive, but they need to be painted and sealed every few years. When they inevitably rot after being in contact with soil, sun, and rain, boards will need replacing. If you haven't got that spacing right then, your fence will lean or fall over. Privacy hedges are a great alternative which adds beauty and is suitable for boosting the area. They add color and texture to your home's exterior, while at the same time blocking your yard from view and mutating unwanted noise.

As you think about the look you want for your garden, there are several variations in hedges to consider. Landscaping can determine your yard's aesthetics, so you'll want to decide whether a more informal or formal looks the most desirable. Think about choosing bushes such as the blue- or pink-flowered hydrangea or the striking rhododendron for an informal privacy haven. Consider the majestically sweet bay or the lovely white-trimmed leaves of the evergreen euonymus for a more formal, trimmed hedge. If you're looking for something irregular or unique, bamboo may be an option. There are two bamboo types: jumping and clumping. The running types fill in quickly but must be contained so that they don't accidentally wander their way into your neighbor's yard, while the clumping variety grows slower and is more shrub like.

You'll want to choose an evergreen shrub for the highest degree of privacy. Unlike the deciduous varieties, evergreens won't drop their leaves in the winter. They have lush privacy year-round. The blue holly grows 5-12 feet tall. It has glittering leaves, sprouts beautiful red berries and grows in partial shade or full sun. You might want to look at the grape from Oregon too. This bush has something to it all. It grows to a 6 feet height, sprouts small, yellow flowers and produces an edible blue-black fruit. It loves the sun and can be trimmed or left in its natural state into a formal hedge.

It depends on where you live to choose the right bush, the look you want for your yard and the area you need to fill. Hedges come in all shapes and sizes, and you may want to seek guidance from a landscaping professional. A professional can help you design your dreams' privacy hedge and help shape your living "fence" into smooth shapes, incorporating the best color mix for you.

CHAPTER 2
Paint Your Picture with Plants

This advanced cultivating theory plays an intermediary in the landscape, putting plants in a spot where they'll generally flourish — with negligible contribution from the plant specialist. The outcome is a landscape configuration that is a breeze to keep up.

Advantages of Right Plant, Right Place

When you put the correct plant in the perfect spot, giving it almost perfect developing conditions, a few things occur:

Plants set up rapidly, developing and building up

Plants produce robust root frameworks and consistent top development

Plants withstand an assault by creepy crawlies and sicknesses. Plants in an inappropriate spot have an undermined safe framework, maybe, and when a bug comes, they're ready for the contaminating.

The most significant venture you'll make when you tackle right plant, opportune spot cultivating happens before you stick trowel into the soil. Arranging is the way to progress with this idea. By contributing additional time before planting, you'll contribute less time looking after plantings. You'll be cultivating more brilliant and greener — and setting aside cash, as well.

Start with Hardiness Zone

Numerous plant specialists push the envelope on the solidness zone and develop plants from one zone hotter. They fold these sketchy survivors into a shielded terrace or possibly in a planting bed close to a southern mass of their home, where temperatures don't fall very as far in winter. Without a doubt, achievement, however, fill a landscape configuration using plants that are solid to your zone.

Stock Light

A few plants require full sun to thrive; many need shades. Once you know what kind of light your yard provides, you will get the best seeding results. To make sense of this, watch the sun as it enters your landscaped territories on a day when you're alone. Check it accurately in a perfect world-and make notes. Therefore, if a plant label says "incomplete shade," you'll know if your yard is meeting certain conditions.

Talk of Soil

Plants have to cultivate specific types of soil to their advantage. The great thing about soil is that you can transform it by making changes. For example, by adding natural problems, similar to compost, you can render clay soil, which is moderately depleting, gradually permeable, and quicker depleting. Or on the other hand, by building and filling raised beds, you can produce a totally extraordinary soil type in your landscape, which also adds some clever hardscaping to the landscape.

When you place an inappropriate plant in an

incorrect kind of soil, you will get mixed results. The plant bites the dust for the direst outcome imaginable. Best of all, it endures, but with dull performances. Each kind of soil needs an alternate plant palette. Consider the kinds of plants that grow in the soil you have before you set out to make an improvement in the soil. You will discover that you can design a landscape that catches your eye.

Plan Things Up

Plant labels say how big plants grow in ideal conditions. Plan for this possibility and site plants as needed, giving them enough room for covering and plenty of headspace for portability upwards.

Tall plants may form a safety screen in the ideal location, or set up a striking environment for different plantings. They're a blemish on an undesirable spot. On the other side, through encompassing plantings or hardscaping, plants that are too small may be overshadowed and vanish from sight.

Color and texture take over

Consider shading the leaves and blooms as you pick plants, and how it may blend or clash with established landscape and hardscaping. An easy approach to win with shading is to schedule tints from a family with identical shading. This works exceptionally well in front yard gardens, where an excellent first contact with visitors and bystanders is required.

Another technique for goof-confirmation is to dissipate clusters of a similar shading in planting areas, allowing what is known as shading reverberation. Throughout the planting season, note to consider blossom time and prepare for shading. Include differentiating leaf and plant surfaces in the landscape to blend some of the displays.

Outmaneuver Fauna

Most planters are aware of a problem with a critter. Whether it's burrowing voles, leaping hares or wandering deer, untamed life will make any landscape design work short, turning planting efforts into stems and stubble. Although you are most likely unable to win any war, you can outfox the creatures. Similar to a fence, installing hardscaping gives a physical barrier that can restrict the intrusion of untamed life into the planting zones. Be that as it may, a fence is not generally down to earth or reasonable informal front yards or in exorbitantly huge patios.

By choosing plants that they dislike, you can also outmaneuver criteria. If hares eat the coralbells (despite not consuming them), dump the coralbells for anything neighborhood rabbits find less appetizing. You'll save yourself long stretches of frustration over the long term, and potentially a wad of money you'd spend on replacement plants.

Selection of The Plants

These green living things add excellence to your garden as well as will likewise be useful to make a new and sound condition. Before you start with your landscape, make sure that you will have the option to pick the correct plants for it.

1. **Choose where to put the plants.**

One thing that you have to consider in picking plants is where you will put them. If you choose to put plants on the front yard, you need to mind the neighbor's environmental factors with the goal that your yard will complement their yards. This will make your front yard look increasingly wonderful. Ensure that when picking plants, you pick those that will add a bid to your home, and they ought not to cover your home's façade. For the terrace, you have more opportunities on what sort of plants to put since it is a progressively private spot.

2. Know plants' appearance when develops.

You don't merely get whatever plants you can consider. You need to check how they will look if they become developed. Some may become huge and might possess your whole garden. Thus, if you get plants that way, you will be with apprehension to see them gobbling up a gigantic piece of your garden. You additionally need to perceive how tall they can get. If they develop incredibly tall, they may cover your home's front zone. Make sure to pick plants in view of their appearance.

3. Plant hues.

Attempt to envision the sort of garden you need. Do you need it to be beautiful? Or then again, you may just need little flies of shading? Or, on the other hand, you may need it to have all greens in it? Subsequent to settling on the shading, you can pick plants that would suit your taste when we talk about plant hues.

4. Think about soil, climate, and daylight.

Besides those referenced, you likewise need to mind plants that develop in your general vicinity. There are plants that are delicate to daylight and effectively wilt. Spot them in shades. There are plants that develop well in soils that are damp or sort wet. There are likewise plants that flourish with a particular sort of climate. In light of these elements, you will have the option to get the correct plant for you.

5. Get common plants.

Typical plants are those that can develop in your general vicinity with low support. This is useful for the individuals who abhor planting yet couldn't want anything more than to have a good landscape. You can get some ground cover plants or some evergreen growth or anything that would not require additional consideration.

6. Landscape trees.

Using landscape trees in planning your garden is a smart thought. However, you need to know the highlights you need for a tree with the end goal for you to pick the correct one. You can attempt evergreen trees, for they generally keep their foliage even in winter. In picking a tree, think about the tallness, width, shade of leaves, flowers, the shade of leaves, and screening highlights.

7. Evergreen bushes.

Like the evergreen trees that we have referenced in the past passage, evergreen bushes additionally keep their leaves throughout the entire year. Be that as it may, there are blossoming and non-flowering bushes. Choose if you need those that bear flowers or just those that only have left.

8. Deciduous bushes.

In contrast to evergreen plants, deciduous bushes lose their leaves in winter. What you will see is their fanning design, which additionally looks great during winter. You additionally need to choose if you will get flowering or non-blossoming ones.

What is acceptable with these sorts of plants is that they produce exquisite flowers and their leaves can likewise come in beautiful hues during the season like rosy shades.

9. Perennial plants.

You can likewise add some perennial plants to your garden. Perennial plants involve lesser regions, which means you can put them in gatherings or even join various types in a single spot. Along these lines, you can include hues, statures, and surfaces to your garden. A few perennials blossom flowers in various seasons. That is the reason; you need to keep an eye on them, so you will perceive how their flowers resemble. Or then again consolidate various perennials so you will get different sorts of flowers in various seasons.

10. Groundcovers.

Groundcovers add excellence to a landscape. It covers a broad region in the ground. Groundcovers are additionally either evergreen or deciduous and blossoming or non-flowering. Pick which one you would use for your garden. You likewise need to keep an eye on the territory where you will put groundcovers, so you will know whether they will flourish in it. Some are delicate to daylight, while others develop well if they get well more often than not.

Well, getting plants for your landscape is truly not about excellence. You need to think about these green colleagues on how they can live in your general vicinity. Additionally, you need to ensure that they are very much dealt with. Subsequent to picking your plants, the time has come to design your garden.

CHAPTER 3
Landscape Care: Fertilizers, Weeds, Watering

Fertilizers

Plant nutrition is oftentimes the "Goldilocks" of garden decisions; what is too much, what is too little, and what is just right? Fortunately, you have decades of research to guide your garden fertilization decisions. One of the most essential gardening tips is that different crops produce best with different fertilization practices. Therefore, fertilization is not a one-size-fits-all practice; it should be adjusted based on the crops the gardener plans to grow. Furthermore, improper fertilization can lead to pest and disease problems in the garden. It is important to understand the basics of garden fertilization and follow the advice of experts to ensure your garden is nourished "just right."

Micronutrients

Micronutrients are nutrients that plants require in trace quantities. Usually micronutrients are available to plants via weathered rock in the soil. The nine essential micronutrients for plant growth include: iron, manganese, zinc, copper, boron, molybdenum, nickel, cobalt, and chlorine. Gardeners only need to add micronutrients upon evidence of a nutrient deficiency. Nutrient deficiencies can be difficult to diagnose correctly. If a gardener suspects a nutrient deficiency, USU Extension advises that gardeners submit a sample of the affected plant to their local Extension office for diagnosis. The most common micronutrient deficiency in Utah soils is iron chlorosis. Sufficient iron is present in Utah soils; however, due to local soil chemistries, it is tied up in a form that is unavailable for plants. Treatment options for iron chlorosis include amendment of garden soil with organic matter, adopting appropriate watering practices, and the addition of iron chelates or sequestered iron products. Note that one cannot bury iron nails or artifacts in the soil to treat symptoms of iron chlorosis. Chelated or sequestered iron products are costly but are the only appropriate additive other than organic matter for treatment of iron chlorosis. Chelated iron products must be re-applied over time to maintain management of iron chlorosis.

Fertilizer Applications

Fertilizer applications should be calculated based on the analysis on the fertilizer bag. Any fertilizer can be substituted for another fertilizer choice. For example, ammonium sulfate (21-0-0) can be substituted for other organic or inorganic nitrogen sources. If you prefer to use urea (46-0-0), you would use approximately half the fertilizer amount compared to ammonium sulfate (21-0-0) because urea contains approximately twice the amount of nitrogen (46 percent) as ammonium sulfate (21 percent). If you prefer to use an organic nitrogen fertilizer, like hoof/horn meal (12-2-0), you would use twice as much fertilizer as compared to ammonium sulfate since hoof/horn meal contains approximately half the amount of nitrogen (12 percent) compared to ammonium sulfate (21 percent). Note that organic fertilizers tend to release nutrients more slowly than fast-release inorganic nitrogen fertilizers. Therefore, rapid-release organic nitrogen fertilizers should be selected or the slow-release organic nitrogen fertilizer should be allowed more time to dissipate as compared to a fast-release nitrogen fertilizer source. For a listing of organic fertilizers and

Watering

One of the top contributors to plant problems in Northern Utah is over-watering, despite the fact that Utah is the second driest state in the United States. Utahns cannot rely on Mother Nature for adequate garden moisture and therefore must irrigate vegetable and fruit crops because we live in a semiarid climate. Unfortunately Utahns often make poor judgments when determining how much and how often to water their landscapes. Plant roots require both water and oxygen to grow. Therefore, if the soil is constantly saturated with water, there is no room left in soil pore spaces to house gases like oxygen. This situation likely results in weakened health of the plant due to rotting root hair tips. Consequently, the plant may show signs of desiccation due to its inability to take up water through the damaged root hairs. Plants in a weakened or stressed state are more susceptible to pest and disease attacks. In this sense, plants are much like humans. If you are experiencing extreme levels of stress and not caring for your body through proper sleep, diet, and exercise, you are more prone to becoming sick.

Impact of Watering

Most plant problems are a result of multiple factors. Gardeners may be able to see a tree borer or blossom end rot visually, but these conditions may be partially explained by other factors like inconsistent watering which left the plant susceptible to the visual symptoms. These are tough facts for many gardeners, who like to think they know best and would never do anything to stress garden plants. The harsh reality, however, is that Mother Nature never lies. Physical symptoms show evidence of plant stress; gardeners should step back and take a critical look at the care of the plant before assuming the culprit of the stress had nothing to do with the care of the plant.

Plants are like humans in another sense; they prefer consistency. Change is hard in our lives and often brings about stress. Plants share our disdain for change. Plants, of course, do not "feel" like humans do, however, drastic changes in moisture, temperature, or other growing conditions are difficult for them.

Therefore, inconsistent watering is enormously stressful on plants. The natural reaction to letting a plant dry out too much is to keep it well hydrated. This fluctuation of care is actually more difficult on plants than the original stress. The original stress of drying out likely caused the plant to respond to the dry conditions physiologically. If dry conditions are followed by a period of too much moisture, an additional stress might be placed on an already weakened plant.

Weeds

Weed control in the vegetable garden is often a source of constant frustration for many gardeners. Some gardeners cope with constant weed seed germination by acknowledging that the garden will never be weed-free; rather weeds should be controlled throughout the growing season. A stepping stone made by a talented USU Extension Master Gardener reads "all my weeds are wildflowers." Although weeds are plants like crops and oftentimes present a beautiful flower, they compete with fruit and vegetable crops for water and nutrients. In this sense, weeds are unwelcome inhabitants in the garden. However, in some cases, weeds provide benefits, too. For example, some flowering weeds like dandelions provide a consistent nectar and pollen source for bees.

Weed Identification

Just like pest and disease control, weeds must first be correctly identified to be properly controlled. Weeds can be annual (like redstem filaree), biennial (like bull thistle), or perennial (like field bindweed). By knowing the life cycle of a weed and its method of reproduction, a savvy gardener can get to the root of effective weed control. For example, annual weeds must re-seed themselves annually to survive. Therefore, it is a gardener's goal to prevent an annual weed from reseeding itself by preventing the seedlings from germinating or by controlling seedlings before they produce mature seed. Perennial weeds come back for 3 or more years and therefore require additional control techniques. Gardeners often target the root system of perennial weeds.

Preventative Weed Control

Weed control can be accomplished in the garden using multiple techniques. The best technique for weed control is prevention. Like Integrated Pest Management (IPM), steps should be taken early in the growing season to prevent excessive weed growth. USU Extension receives many phone calls from Utahns frustrated with battling weeds in the garden. Upon asking the caller questions about care of the garden, it becomes obvious that the gardener did not take precautionary measures to inhibit weed growth early in the growing season. Preventative weed control is an investment that will reward you with less weeding later in the growing season. Examples of preventative strategies include mulching, pre-emergent herbicide use, and maintenance of a dense ground cover to out-compete weeds.

Mulching

Mulching can help reduce weed growth by restricting light from reaching weed seeds. Several materials can be used as mulch including organic mulches like wood chips or straw and inorganic mulches like black or clear plastic. Fabric  mulch, commonly called weed barrier cloth, can also be used to control weeds. Organic mulches, such as shredded bark or wood chips, will slowly break down and supply nutrients to plants, whereas plastic mulches and weed barrier cloth do not decompose and may obstruct soil formation under the mulch layer. Clear plastic mulch can be  used to solarize the soil by heating the soil surface and "cooking" weed seeds in the top few inches of soil.

Mechanical Weed Control

Even with our best efforts, every garden will still grow weeds. Mechanical weed control is a low impact, environmentally safe way to control weeds. Weeds can be controlled by hoeing, cultivating, mulching, or hand weeding. It is important to remove the weed before the plant has the opportunity to flower and produce seed. Weed seeds should not be placed in the backyard compost bin. Try to remove as much of the weed as possible. For example, some perennial weeds, like dandelions, have a long taproot that grows deep into the garden soil. If a gardener were to pull the dandelion and snap the plant off at the soil surface, the taproot would almost certainly flush out new leaves and flowers. Weeds with long taproots should be removed with a weed pick, preferably at a time when the soil is moist and soft to facilitate the gardener in extracting the entire plant. Smaller weeds are typically easier to control than mature weeds.

Chemical Weed Control

The use of herbicides can be an effective tool for weed control. Herbicides may be classified as pre-emergent (inhibiting weed seed germination), broad spectrum (killing all plants), selective (only killing certain types of plants), or organic herbicides. Furthermore, herbicides can be contact (only affecting contacted tissue) or systemic (entering and moving throughout a plant). Herbicides can be difficult to use in a small garden setting due to the close proximity of vegetable plants to the weeds. One common injury is herbicidal drift injury which occurs when droplets of herbicide drift with the breeze and settle on non-targeted vegetable plants. Drift commonly occurs when herbicides are applied at too high of pressures.

CHAPTER 4
How to Enhance Your Garden with Pots, Containers, Raised Bed?

There are many reasons to garden in a raised bed or in containers. In fact, some people think they are unfortunate not to have a lot of land to cultivate but to be honest, they may be better off.

That's not an exaggeration.

Sure, if you find good land, then raised beds and containers can't compete, but good land isn't that common anymore in urban and suburban areas. Here are some reasons why you may not want to plant in-ground.

Reasons to Avoid Planting In-Ground

- **Poor Soil Structure** - Have you ever tried planting a tree in rocky, clay soil? I have and it's not exactly easy. Instead of a shovel, a pickaxe would have been more useful. Not only is such soil difficult to work with, even with a tiller, but it will probably have other problems such as poor drainage and low organic matter. On the flip side, you could have soil that drains too well. Extremely sandy soils are problematic because they readily leach nutrients and hold little moisture. Problems with soil structure can often be solved by adding plenty of organic matter like compost, but that can be a lot of work if your planned garden is large and you don't have a tiller on hand.

- **Existing Pests In-Ground** - It is recommended that root crops not be planted in first-year gardens that have been converted from lawn. The reason being that soil-dwelling grubs are likely in the soil and will feed on your crops. Existing nematodes also have a possibility of being harmful to your plants and large pests, like voles, can be a real nuisance. Because these problems exist in the ground, they are also difficult to treat.

- **Weeds, Grass, and Roots** - Every garden is susceptible to weeds. The seeds can be blown into a raised garden or container the same way in can be blown along the ground. However, raised beds and containers are much less susceptible to weeds that spread vegetative, such as Bermuda grass. Also, when it comes to spreaders, it's hard not to mention tree and shrub roots. These wide spreaders can extend several yards away from the main plant and will suck water and nutrients away from other plants. Root crops are especially vulnerable to these effects.

- **Flooding** - Even sandy soil can flood if there is enough rain. Many people have the impression that flooding is only a problem if the water persists, but the truth is that even brief flooding can devastate a garden. If you have seedlings or newly planted seeds, a flood event can ruin everything. Small plants can be beaten down into the mud and catch disease while seeds that have yet to germinate can get washed away. Leafy greens can also get severely contaminated if the flood waters mix with waste water or roadway runoff. In fact, it is recommended to discard all leafy greens if they are caught in flood waters and cook vegetables that could have been contaminated. That includes things normally eaten raw, like strawberries.

- **Bad Location** - Where your soil is may not be where plants like to grow or it could be too far from your water source. Of the many things you can work around, the sun is one of the most difficult. If your ground area gets too little sun, you can work around that by placing raised beds/containers in the sunny spots that you do have even if they are on top of hard surfaces.

Any of those issues can be enough to ruin the garden and some places can actually fall victim to every single one. While you probably have a good idea of the benefits raised gardens and containers have, I want to go over some more unique properties that make them desirable.

Benefits of Raised Beds and Container

• **Fresh Soil** - Building a raised garden allows you to formulate a soil that has all the properties plants like and none of the things that may restrict them. People often use this opportunity to create a rich growing mix that is high in organic matter.

• **Fast Temperature Change** - Having a smaller volume than the ground, containers and raised beds are more susceptible to temperature changes. This feature makes the soil warm faster and allows for slightly earlier planting than in-ground plants. With crops like sweet potato that need warm soil, this can add several weeks to the growing season. Caution must be taken though, as containers can heat up too much in direct sunlight and also freeze earlier in Winter.

- **Ability to Sterilize** - With containers, if your plants contract a soil-borne disease or pest, you can easily discard the growing mix, sterilize the container, and add fresh soil. This can also eliminate the need to rotate crops and allow you to grow plants like potatoes every year. Technically, you don't have to discard soil and can sterilize it by baking in an over, but I find that too impractical for home gardeners.

- **Easy to Shelter** - Growing a tropical plant and having to dig it up every Winter can be a hassle. Too much of a hassle for most gardeners. However, keeping such plants restricted to containers makes their movement and storage simple and easy.

- **Better Accessibility** - Gardening can be hard work. From weeding to harvesting, bending down is a constant requirement when everything is at ground-level. Raised beds and even containers make such tasks easier. Even if it's just a foot or two off the ground, that can be enough for some to tell a difference. If you don't believe me, touch your toes. Notice the difference in physical strain those last few inches make. Raised beds can be built high to allow people with major disabilities to garden comfortably and containers can be place on tables.

- **Aesthetics** - Many people regard raised beds and containers more aesthetically pleasing compared to a standard garden. What you decide to use can ultimately be a design element for your landscape.

A whiskey barrel planter filled with flowers is a powerful focal piece compared to if those flowers were just placed in the ground. The added vertical appeal does a lot to bring a space alive. However, a raised bed or container garden can quickly get out of hand and look disorganized if you aren't careful.

Creating an in-ground garden is certainly quicker and often cheaper than doing raised beds or containers, but it's not always the best option. It's important to consider your space, the plants you want to grow, the tools available, and your budget when deciding how you want to construct your garden.

Water gardening is a very beautiful style of gardening, which has been around for years and followed. In addition, the Mughal gardens were built with outdoor spaces. Water brings life to all organisms, whatever their size might be.

CHAPTER 5
How to Build A to Give More Charm to Your Garden?

Simulation of a natural ecosystem with a body of water is called water gardening through diligent maintenance utilizing the different plants and other devices. It helps in breaking a great land scape's daily grind. Such styles of gardens are common in traditional gardening design. The water gardens have an infinite variety of selections, layout and planting make them unique and customized in their style. In comparison to the Mughal model of gardens, the Japanese architecture of the garden also allows the use of the water dimension as a very significant feature of their lawns as well as the koi fishes inside it.

In the water field, the plants are easy to grow. The plant species in a water garden were either completely deeply embedded in the ground or float on the surface of the water, or may even be submerged. The rooted plants may either be planted directly into the soil, or they can be planted in small containers and put on the earth's surface. The creation of shelf-like constructions during the development of a water garden is crucial for those

plants being placed in the pots. There are no problems with the floating plants, and they can float in the water surface.

The larger the water garden, the better the opportunities for the plants and the different technologies that are built into the water garden.

Soil is added to a length of about 1 foot before planting the deeply ingrained plants, and manures such as compost or cow dung are added to ensure the plants grow well. Rooted plants are grown, and water is filled up to the crown area.

What are Those Constituents?

Pond liners — Such help in building an artificial region of water. The liners are produced from a range of materials, including cotton, fiberglass, plastics, and concrete. If the liners set the essential framework for the water garden, then the fixing. They come in different shapes and sizes.

Pumps — In a water field, whether in a pool, whether field waterfalls, it helps to transfer power from one fluid through another. It also serves to improve the water quality by treating it.

Filters — Used for the sole purpose of washing water at the water plant. The sensors can be either mechanical or biological. The water simply moves through the tank in the water garden and is filtered by this process. It's keeping plants and fish healthier in the atmosphere. Skimmers are a sort of electronic device that purifies the greater water waste.

Fountains — They render a truly beautiful feature in the water garden. They break the monotony of water-gardening. The several various styles of the fountain and the specific lighting bring charm to the whole garden

Waterfall — The waterfalls provide a calm and serene atmosphere for the water garden, and it is aesthetically pleasing too. The gentle waterfall audio provide a calming impact on the people there.

Lightings — Used to optimize the attractiveness of the different technologies added to the water plant.

Planning & Construction of Water Gardens

A water garden offers many possibilities to plant and grow. You can start small, with a boiled-out stone trying to collect in-ground storage tank, a watertight, patio-sized vessel, or dive in with a lily, fish, and shower right in. Do some research before you create a water garden to assess your severity and style? Unlike conventional gardening, where nearly every job can be skipped and fresh resumed sometime next year, there are more room and resources in a field. A smaller container water garden, without losing the soothing elegance and color of water plants, can be a great fit for your health and individual finances.

1. Design & Setup

If you plan on building the in-ground basin, please feel free to contact an existing local contractor or review the options and requirements carefully before starting. Faults may be onerous, and a lack of preparation. Here's a rundown of what's required while creating a reservoir. A natural-looking liquid garden will have sloping sides with planting terraces that descend to the lower portion of the pond. So, to build various habitats, you should grow a range of plant produce. For northern areas, a depth of 24 to 36 inches is typically needed to ensure that the pond does not ice tightly for winter.

2. Disposable Pots

Imagine a smaller-scale water ground at the garden, conveniently usable for something. Most water plants can be formed in a water tank on your deck, and you can add fish or a pond to it too. Use a plastic resin-filled bottle of whiskey, or buy a specially built ceramic tub for a water bath. The full-sized water lilies, lotus, as well as several other water plants grow well into as little as up to 20 gallons of fresh water. Place your bowl where you would get a minimum of 6 hours of sunlight a day for improved plant growth and flowering. The cans perform well in hot weather, despite afternoon rain.

3. Simple Soil Gardens

You can make a deep pool from twice the average a container of cheap wine or wine bottle, a hidden aluminum pony trough, a submerged bath (it's edges covered by flat rocks), or even a large plastic bucket When you build a dam, you'll need to be more vigilant about its size than its capability. A shallow pool at the lowest part of the backyard for amphibians, native birds, and other animals will be no less than 18 streams at the yard will have sloping sides such that amphibians can run in and out quickly. Steep sided wetlands, lacking noticeable rocks or trees, can catch frogs and salamanders in the water. If you can't use the underwater liner to build softly sloping sides, put partly underwater rocks or trees in the pool to move animals to and fro the water. When the tub is in a place you'd want it to be sitting all season, fill it halfway over with sandy loam dirt. (No use of fertilizer or other biological material in the soil; water clouding) Gradually let water drip from of the nozzle into the bottle till the bottle is well over half-finished. Fill the bucket with water to the bottom before a few extracts of the plant have been produced and scatter in a gradual trickle as before. We will bring it under the surface if animals think the garden interesting. If you plan a few days later on bringing any fish species into the swimming area, do so.

4. Select a Seat in the Pool

Pools of fauna claim a mixture of shade. Shade can be critical to the hottest time of the day, ensuring this same water would be too hot for plants. A pond needs sunlight in several cases for the photosynthetic procedure and for the production of oxygen. Keep it away from areas prone to runoff, particularly after heavy rainfall. You can be really watchful about using chemicals and other equipment in your household, so users don't always know how much your neighbors are using. Most importantly, make sure you have access to your account here!

5. In a Liners Bowl

The bath is set up in three simple options: plastic shower liners actually performed ponds that could be waterlogged in the earth or natural liner. The pond liners may be expensive, but they're very robust and easy to cover by placing rocks at the top along the bottom of your pond. Pre-formed pools may be simple to handle but don't account for your own unique touch system, size, and sophistication. Even the basic can match clay. This is not inherently a leak-proof device, but this normal replacement would be preferable by some. This works well if you place your ponds inside an area that is already very wet, as it can be easily drained from your pond once the water is extracted.

6. Length of a Pond

Pond levels vary from the owner's view. Consider what the river is going to be used for, and how deep the water has to be for different plants. Water lilies expect to start at depths of 18 to 36 inches, while most other aquatics intend to have three to four feet of precipitation above their tops. 24 to 30 inch deep ponds enable the water to heat up sufficiently for safe plant growth. For some, the depth of a marsh is calculated by security criteria. When younger kids are tried to introduce to the water, both smart advice is given to keep it fuller and to alert them to safety questions. You might want to fence the pond in, or while you love the underwater plants, kids should use life jackets.

7. Marine Seeding Oasis

It is easy to take them out when it is time to rinse the edge of the ocean or put tender plants indoors for winter when all the liquid garden seedlings have been planted in pots. This also streamlines the job of dividing crowded perennials when necessary and prevents aggressive blowers from spreading through the water garden and trying to chase out less offensive plants. Cover the soil with 1⁄2 inch pea gravel or small stones inside the bottles and saturate to water before gradually dropping these same containers into the bath to keep the water from muddying as plants are placed in the pool.

Whether the plants are potted or not, utilize hard potting soil or topsoil without trying to apply perlite or other fillers since they may rise to the top and spoil the garden's look. To avoid commercial potting mixes, as they may involve herbicides or chemicals that can harm fish and other wildlife. Organic waste is often undesirable; the water will break down and become contaminated. Healthy clay soil is well fit for aquatic planting.

8. For Fish

Do not extend the water filter and allow the chloride dissolve in the river until at least three days if a tiny tank of rainwater is full. The bonus of having fish is that it helps to keep your water garden free from bugs and pests and is enjoyable to watch. The drawbacks are that they can ultimately relocate and even consume seeds, fouling the surroundings. By adding a mulch coat over the soil of sunken containers to plants somewhere within them and above the bottom of the tub, you will help stop the bathwater from muddling up.

If you wish to carry fish, you should attach them to your farm about two weeks after the garden was built. Give them raw fish foods until the water supplies enough insect larvae to support their nutritional needs. The others put in their ponds koi (brightly colored carp), or goldfish. This is because these fish are easy to handle, and can tolerate small amounts of dissolved oxygen in tiny ponds. Since pond species are limited, though, and the likelihood of releasing these fish into the wild is low, it is prudent to hold them in your tank.

CHAPTER 6
Different Examples of Landscapes

Landscape Designs for Tropical Areas

The best landscape styles for gardens located in tropical regions are the rustic and low-maintenance styles. This is because the plants required to achieve these styles are appropriate for the tropical climate. You won't have to spend time taking care of these plants since they can readily survive in your area.

The Rustic Style

The plants you need to achieve a rustic landscape are: ferns, vine maple, different varieties of elderberry (e.g. Madonna, Black Lance, Common Native, Black Beauty, etc.), as well as ninebark plants (e.g. Native, Center glow, Diabolo, Coppertiana, etc.).

Get these plants if you want to add a meadow-like feel to your rustic garden:

- Penstemon
- Echiracea plant
- ox-eye daisies
- Rudbeckia nitida plant
- Morning light grass

When using this style, you should try to reflect on the appearance of the natural environment. This principle is particularly important for gardens found in grasslands or woodlands. However, although this kind of style needs to show a "natural" look, you need to know some basic guidelines. These are:

What you should do:

a. Utilize pathways to create "mood-changing" effects – It is best if you will use a wide pathway for the entry point of your garden because it encourages the visitor to walk into the area quickly. The pathway should become narrower inside the garden to slow the person down and let him/her appreciate the landscape.

b. Allow the moss to grow – Moss provides a unique feel to the structures of a rustic landscape. Professionals consider it as excellent addition to this style.

What you should not do:

a. Do not use plants that are available everywhere – You want your landscape to be unique, so stay away from generic garden plants. You may start your own plant collection by checking the ferns and herbs found in your region. Afterwards, include plants that will provide additional texture and multicolored foliage.

Low Maintenance Landscape Design

The plant choices – you have to focus on plants that can survive with minimal care. Hardy evergreen plants are the usual choices of professional landscape artists. When selecting the plants to use, always check their average height and range of foliage. Avoid plants that tend to spread out too wide because you will be required to prune them regularly.

To achieve a great looking low maintenance landscape, you just have to avoid a few things. These are:

a. Mature plants – You may attempt to establish your garden instantly by buying mature plants, but this option often causes maintenance problems. It is best to start your garden with younger plants since they usually require minimal attention.

b. Delicate plants – If you have these plants in your landscape, you will need to move, wrap, and relocate them on a regular basis. This will require time and effort from you, which is against the core principle of the low maintenance style.

Landscape Styles for Cold Regions

Cold climate is great for whimsical and wild styles of landscaping.

The Whimsical Style

When using this style, you need to look for things that can be "repurposed" (e.g. toilets, bathtubs, etc.) They can be used as containers for your plants, and will give your landscape an unusual and interesting effect.

You can also include old garden equipment into your landscape. For example, you can place a beat-up wheelbarrow in one of the corners of your garden and use it as a container for your plants or flowers.

The Wild Style

To ensure that your wild landscape gets everyone's attention, you must use brightly colored flowers and plants with different sizes and textures. Your best options are: peonies, lobelias, boxwood, lavenders and irises.

The only rule that you have to keep in mind is this: always check the height of plants before adding them into your garden. This is important since you are going to use the landscape to create privacy.

Landscape Designs for Dry Areas

Beautiful gardens can be established even in regions with high temperatures and minimal water availability. We will focus on the Desert and Tuscan landscape styles.

Desert Landscape Style

In this landscape design, you should use succulents and plants that are accustomed to hot temperatures. The plants commonly used in this style are:

- Agave
- Cacti
- Sedum
- Aloe
- Yucca

Here are some colorful plants that can survive in your region: yellow columbine, begonia, bunny ears, and autumn sage. You should never attempt to have a lawn when doing this style since that requires regular supply of water.

Agave

Yucca

Tuscan Design

This particular style combines popular plants (e.g. rosemary, lavender, Italian cypress, etc.) and brightly colored items (e.g. natural stones, flowers, and urns).

Here are the plants commonly used by professionals:

- Thyme
- Fig
- Bay
- Citrus
- Olive
- Grape vine
- Italian cypress
- Rosemary
- Lavender

Grasses used as ornaments in the Tuscan style are:

- Moor
- Lindheimer's muhly
- Deer grass

Landscape artists sometimes add these to Tuscan gardens:

- Pearl blue bush
- Mediterranean fan

Different varieties of sage (e.g. bee's bliss, white, Jerusalem, and Cleveland sages).

Landscape Designs for Areas with Moderate Climate

The French Style

When using this style in designing your landscape, you need to include these basic elements:

- Glazed pots
- Fountains
- Concrete balustrade
- Birdbaths
- Antique ornaments
- Natural stones
- Elegant furniture
- Iron seats
- Columns
- Trellises

To ensure that your French garden catches the attention of everyone, keep these things in mind:

Geometry — In designing your garden, everything should be geometric and positioned symmetrically.

Terraces — should be positioned in the garden so that every detail of the landscape can be easily viewed.

Water — is considered as the primary element of this style. Use pools and fountains in oval, rectangular, or circular shapes.

CHAPTER 7
A Patio Garden Provide Privacy and Pleasure Like an Outdoor Living Room

The first thing you need to find out is if you have a preference for straight lines or curves. This may seem like a slightly unusual thing to need to know, but, believe me, it's very important.

It's very easy to start to design a patio with straight lines purely because the paving slabs are very linear. However, if your actual tastes are for curves and the rest of your garden has quite curvy shapes within it, then straight lines aren't necessarily going to be the best option.

One of the key elements in creating a great design is to be unlimited in your thinking about how materials and shapes should be used. Certainly, building a curved patio is more work and will cost a little bit more, but the end results can be amazing and well worth it.

Where to Start with Your Patio Plan

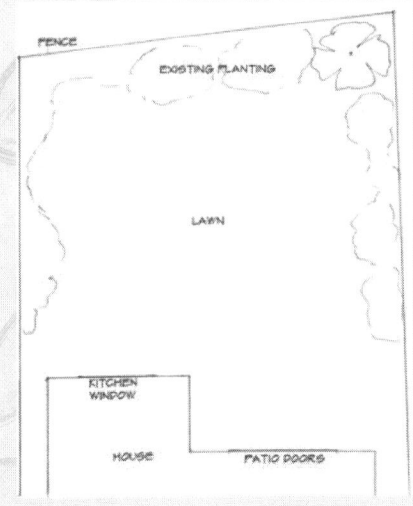

So now you have your base plan, of which you've made several copies so you can try out different designs. The plan should show your house with the position of the doors and windows. It should also show your entire garden with the position of the boundary lines and any plant borders, trees and features that you wish to keep, as shown in the example plan.

You also have information about the position of the sun at different times of the day so that you position the patio in the right area. To begin with, we will assume that the area outside your patio doors is going to be the perfect location for your patio.

Putting Pencil to Paper

It can be a little bit daunting when you have a fairly blank piece of paper staring back at you. But don't worry; I'm going to show you some techniques that will get you past any fear you may have.

Good design is actually really simple. I know that

may sound a little boring, but it's not when it's done properly. If something is overly complicated and showy for the sake of it, it's like somebody wearing too many different styles and colors of clothing with a hundred and one pieces of jewelry. Not usually a good look, is it?

In your mind's eye, compare the person that is wearing so much bling it's making your eyes hurt, to the person in a very classic outfit with one or two pieces of carefully chosen jewelry. Which is the most attractive?

The First Design Step

With a pencil, draw either a semi-circle, square, rectangle or any other simple geometric shape to represent your patio. Don't think too much about this, just draw something, anywhere that feels right.

Also, do not judge what you have drawn, not yet. Designing is a mixture of left-brained, free-flowing creativity and right-brained logical thought. Don't worry if you think you're not creative. We all are to a greater or lesser degree; you just may not be used to using that side of your brain as much.

Play Time!

The scribble technique works because your brain zones out whilst you scribble, just like a five-year-old does. As children, we are all very creative.

Unfortunately, as adults, we tend to judge ourselves too harshly and end up blocking this ability.

So when you do this, it's really important not to judge yourself or to worry if you've got things in the right place. Pretend you are five again and just scribble away. Accept that you won't get things in the right place, not on your first go, and you will need to adjust and modify things; it's just part of the process.

Designing Logically

Now that the scribble part of the process is out the way, you need to think more logically about what it is you're trying to achieve. If you don't know what needs to be different after doing the scribble technique, that's OK, don't worry; this next part will help you to progress.

Try to think about these key things:

1. Do you want your patio area to be open or secluded?
2. Which doors do you need to access the most from the patio?
3. Which windows do you look out to your garden from the most?
4. Is there a change in the level that needs to be taken into account?
5. What is the best position for any furniture or features, such as a barbecue?

If you want your patio area to be secluded, you can use screening like trellis, planting or railings. But it's important that you do not block off the views from your house too much, otherwise the patio will look small and could feel quite claustrophobic.

Think about your main access door across the patio and make sure that with all the furniture and features you intend to put on the patio, there is good access to your main route of passage. Nothing is more annoying than constantly having to side-step around tables and chairs and not being able to get where you want to go quickly and easily. Never mind it being a tripping hazard for kids.

How to Incorporate Changes in Level into Your Design?

The simpler you can make the transition from one level to another, the better it will be. Some patio designs on the Internet are overly complicated with changes in level. Whilst that might add some interest, it's really not a good idea for every day, practical use.

If at all possible, try to avoid changes in level in the main patio area itself. This is particularly important if you want to set out table and chairs. You want to avoid someone toppling over when they move their chair back.

If you do have to incorporate a level change in the patio, make sure you line it up with a house wall

so that it is an obvious level change. See the diagram below.

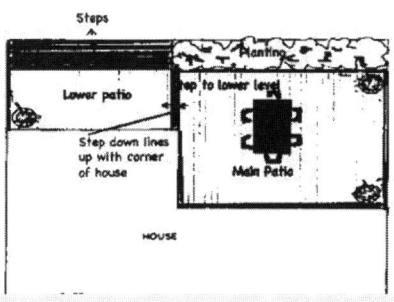

Level change lining up with corner of the house

You may think level changes are obvious, and it doesn't matter if it's in the middle of the patio or not, but when you watch small children, the elderly and new visitors, it can make quite uncomfortable viewing seeing them navigate level changes they are not expecting.

However, the very best way to tackle changes in level is with the use of steps, either before or after the main patio. Having steps leading up or down to the patio from the house is much easier on a practical and visual level. It will enable you to avoid unexpected level changes.

It is much better if you have a step immediately outside your patio doors, or at the end of the patio, than to have it in the middle. To begin with, though, just concentrate on getting the overall shape of your patio right before you start on level changes.

Trying to do too much in one go makes designing difficult. So just take it one bit at a time. Get the overall shape first, then work out how you get from A to B with the level changes, and adjust your patio shape accordingly.

Designing With Different Levels

If there is a change in level, where is the best position for the steps? It can look and feel nice if the width of the steps lines up and matches the width of your patio doors or your main window for example.

To create a more open feel to your patio, you could run the width of the steps down the entire length of your patio and this will really help to blend your patio and garden in with the house as shown in the picture below.

Another aspect of safety, especially if the patio is raised above the height of the rest of the garden, is railings or a balustrade. These are necessary, as you don't want to take the risk of people inadvertently falling off your patio. However, they can obscure the view to the rest of the garden, if you're not careful.

One solution is to create a physical barrier without creating too much of a visual one. Using timber with stainless steel straining wire will make quite a

modern looking balustrade. Metal railings will also work as they don't usually need to be as thick as wooden balustrades. The less you visually obscure the rest of the garden, the larger the space will feel.

CHAPTER 8
Garden Geometry Transform A Small Front Yard

The landscape design of the front yard is an integral part of developing an overall outdoor layout that truly shows the beauty of your home. Landscape design makes the most of your real estate.

Your design of the landscape starts as soon as the it connects to your driveway and continues in your space outside. At the same time, your front yard's landscaping will set the tone for the rest of your exterior design.

Using trees, shrubbery and flowers to accentuate your front yard

Plant life and vegetation are a critical part of most

landscapes and are just as important to your front yard as ever. Choosing plants and flowers which complement your garden style and your home style is essential. There are a few other tips to keep in mind when creating a plan for planting your landscape design at the front yard.

Trees

- Big trees are great summer heat relief and can help to cool your home when it's properly planted.

- Smaller trees, such as citrus trees and fruit trees, or ornamentals such as crepe myrtles, give color and often give a sweet aroma.

- Ornamental and fruit trees are often planted in lines to accentuate drives or create a living boundary along with the estate.

Shrubbery

Depending on the style of your garden, evergreen shrubs, boxwoods, and classy topiaries are an ideal way to add texture to the landscape design of your front yard.

- Often the shrubs are used to create patterns and direction.

- These plant types can make excellent hedges too.

Flowers

A number of landscape designs for year-round color depend on a variety of seasonal perennials, mixed with a variety of evergreens. Flowers can make your front yard bright and inviting while creating in your outdoor space a number of visual effects. Choose colors that compliment your current use of colors and consider these tips for planting:

- For a recessed, distant appearance, use calming shades, like green or blue.
- bright hues, such as yellow and red, draw attention and will accentuate parts of your yard that need to be highlighted.
- Design flower beds around the edge of your home and along paths and hiking tracks.
- Fill empty space with lush grass which can be functional as well as beautiful.

Other elements of landmark design at the front yard

While the back of your home may only be seen by family and friends as a primarily private area, your front yard plays a major role in defining the appearance of your entire property. In addition to the plant life you choose, there are several different ways to add to your front yard and increase your home's curb appeal.

Front Yard Hardscape Design — Paths and driveways may be a necessity, but the way they are designed and designed can have a major impact on your landscape. Choose materials that suit your landscape theme, and use clear lines and curves to accentuate the overall look and feel of your house. Plan drives which make it easier to get to your home. Circular driveways have a quick entry and exit or can be built into a conventional straight drive with an open area to turn around.

Courtyards' Appeal — often enclosed with walls or fencing; courtyards are attractive features because they provide an intimate seating, relaxing and entertaining area. Courtyard design requires close attention to lighting and layout, so many homeowners depend on a professional designer's services.

Your front yard landscape design is the defining factor in the curb appeal of your property from the driveway design to the front porch decor and reflects the overall look and feel of your property. A professionally landscaped front yard can ensure that your home is made the most of the design.

CHAPTER 9
What Are the Essential Tools That You Need?

One of the best ways to save time in the garden is to use the right tool for the right job. Trying to shape a hedge with hand clippers or loppers will take you forever. Using shears or a power hedge trimmer will make quick, efficient work of the project.

There are so many tools to choose from that the decision can be almost paralyzing. You need a set of loppers, but do you choose bypass or anvil, short or long handles? The short answer is that probably any combination of the above choices will get the job done although some combinations may be better suited to your needs than others. Consider how you want to use the tool and tailor your choice to that purpose.

Hand Tools

The Tool Bucket

One of the biggest time savers I have is my trusty bucket full of my most used tools. I keep it on the back porch ready to grab as I come out the door. The bucket of tools will save you tons of time with no more running back and forth to the shed or garage to get a forgotten tool.

Gardening gloves

The first order of business is protecting your hands. Working in the dirt with bare hands can result in dry, cracked skin, the soil just seems to suck the moisture right out of my skin. Scratches, punctures and broken nails are also common byproducts of bare hands. A nice pair of gardening gloves is pretty much a necessity at my house. There are jobs where I need the dexterity of bare hands, but I wear my gloves as much as possible.

I use a washable pair of gloves with a nitrile coating on the palms and fingers. Washable is very important as, if you are anything like me, you are going to get downright muddy occasionally. Then you wipe your face with your hand and .... ick. The nitrile coating semi-waterproofs and strengthens the fabric. I like gloves with fabric on the backs to let my hands breath.

Trowel

A good quality trowel is a definite requirement. My trowel is my most used tool, hands down. Don't go to the Dollar Store for this particular tool. Those cheap trowels will bend into a pretzel as soon as you put any significant pressure on the handle. You need something that is very sturdy, won't rust and feels good in your hand.

Nippers and Clippers

The next two tools in my arsenal are nippers and clippers. They are my primary tools for deadheading, shaping plants, removing  wayward branches, etc. I use them constantly, all summer long. Because they will get so much use, quality is strongly recommended. You want

 something that will perform year after year with little to no care. You aren't saving time if your tool breaks half-way through the job.

Dandelion Weeder

In case you are wondering "What the heck is a dandelion weeder?", the answer is it is a straight, thin tool about 12" long with a pronged fork at one end and a handle at the other. It is wonderful for taking out weeds with long straight roots such as dandelions and button weed. I have lots of both of those weeds, so my weeder gets lots of use. Be sure to buy a sturdy one as bendable weeders are bound for the garbage in a hurry.

Scissors

Here is where I will advocate for using a cheap, disposable tool. I carry around a set of Dollar Store scissors in my kit. They are great for grabbing if you need to clip off chives or cut back a small, fluffy grass or fern.

I do have a quality pair of garden scissors that can be taken apart for sharpening. They are sturdier than my one-dollar wonders which comes in handy sometimes. I find myself gravitating to the cheaper pair of scissors though whenever possible as they are quick and easy-to-replace and I can be a little careless with them.

Plastic Drinking Cup

Nope, the cup isn't for drinking. I use a cheap plastic drinking cup inside my tool bucket to corral all my small hand tools. The cup will hold the scissors, nippers, clippers and other tiny tools upright so that they are easy to find and grab. No digging around in the bottom of the bucket to find those nippers only to poke your finger on the tip in the process. Having tools that lock closed will make them small enough to fit into the cup with all their buddies easily.

Loppers

I carry two loppers in my tool bucket, short as well as long handled. They are the next step up from clippers in cutting strength. You can take on branches from 1/4" to about 3/4" in diameter with these puppies. Branches larger than that call for a saw of some sort. They are very helpful for fall cutback and for cleaning up and shaping shrubs.

Larger Hand Tools

Shovel

I use my shovel constantly. I keep it standing on the back porch near my bucket of small tools ready to grab as I sweep by headed out to the garden. I use my shovel for so many tasks; planting new perennials, moving mulch or dirt around, digging out those giant weeds that managed to escape the purge, cutting back the roots of plants that are getting too big for their britches, to name just a few. I will even use my shovel as an over-sized trowel to take out huge swathes of weed seedlings by running the blade just under the surface of the soil.

Wheelbarrow

Unless you have a very small garden, you will most likely find yourself in need of a wheelbarrow at some point. I use mine constantly. I use it to transport clippings to the compost pile, to move heavy items around in my garden and occasionally to mix cement in.

Optional Tools for Shrubs and Trees

Bow Saw or Wide-Toothed Tree Saw

When you need to cut a branch that is larger than your loppers can comfortably handle, a saw is the tool you need. I have a bow saw as well as a folding wide-toothed tree saw. Each have their strengths and weaknesses.

Ladder

A sturdy ladder that is quick to set up and take down can be a nice addition to your tool set if you have trees or large shrubs to deal with. You will be much quicker and safer at your pruning with a dependable ladder.

Pole Pruner

A pole pruner can speed up your cutting and shaping activities by allowing you to accomplish more from ground level. A pole pruner is basically a tree saw with a bypass lopper at the base of the saw all attached to a long pole which will be around six feet long. The lopper part will have a hook that allows you to hook it over the branch to be cut. The cutting blade is then pulled up with an attached rope severing the hooked branch.

Power Tools

For those larger yards or ones that require significant pruning or shaping, power tools will save you a huge amount of time. Many of the power tools out there come in two power source options; gasoline based versus rechargeable battery. Your lawn mower should most likely be gas powered unless your lawn is tiny. For any of the other power tools, do your homework. Know what you want to accomplish, how often and how long one use will take.

Mulching Lawnmower

If you have a lawn of any size, you are going to want a power mower. My suggestion is to buy a mulching, power assisted lawnmower. The power assistance will make the pushing easier, but it is an optional nicety. Mulching as you mow is a tremendous time saver. There are no bags to empty and no trails of grass that need to be raked up.

Weed Whacker

The days of the corded weed whackers are long gone (and rightly so). Today your choices revolve around how the whacker is powered and how much brush it can clear. Read reviews and ask around. Buy something that will suit your needs and serve you for many years.

Power Hedge Trimmers

If you love a pretty green hedge, a power hedge trimmer should be on your purchase list. These handy machines make quick work of clipping a hedge into shape. They also are handy for trimming back arbovitae that have grown too big for their britches and are encroaching on other plants. (Perfect for those of you who planted a globe style arb when you really wanted a pillar style. Ahem, guilty as charged.)

CHAPTER 10
Irrigation System

It has been said that water will soon be more valuable than oil. It already is in some parts of the world. We know water will become the number one issue that will shape our landscaping habits in the 21st Century. When water resources begin to dwindle, irrigated landscaping is one of the first things your local providers will restrict to conserve valuable resources. This generally occurs during drought years and unfortunately this coincides exactly with the time we who enjoy our outdoor living space need water the most.

Water collection and irrigation systems work in with planning, hardscapes, and properly draining your area. Water collection and irrigation needs should be considered in your initial plans and once again, the installation of these things will usually require some disruption of the soil; therefore, it is best to do the work before you plant.

Yesterday:

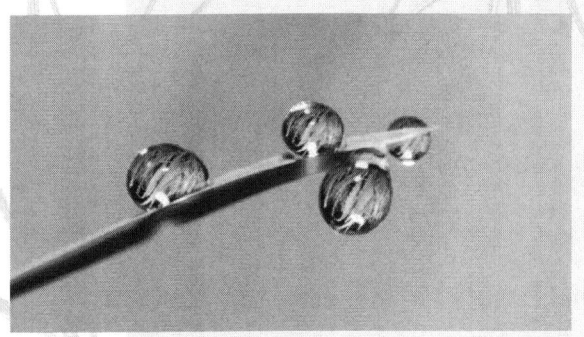

I am certain that water collection goes way back beyond written history. I've already cited several examples that were known from days gone by. I have visited mountain tops and seen pools that were obviously gouged out of solid rock by early Americans. These may have started out as locations to grind seed into edible form. In my part of the country, we refer to these grinding stones as the metate (the bowl shaped receptacle) and mano (the hand-held stone or wood pestle used to grind with). But even as a youngster, it was easy for me to see the practical use these puddles would serve a thirsty Indian up on that mountain top as my dad attempted to explain to me what they were.

The first irrigation tools were likely animal bladders, waterproof baskets, and clay jugs. Western tribes like the Pueblo and Navajos were known to bury clay jugs (called ollas) among their cultivated crops. The unglazed clay would allow water to ooze slowly into the surrounding soil. I consider this to be an early predecessor to drip irrigation. Early cultures did not possess our more sophisticated technology, but they were quite intelligent and resourceful nonetheless.

Water is essential to Life. History shows humanity has been quite capable of maintaining cities and lifestyles that were not so different from our own. We have undeniable proof that we can live without electricity, oil, coal, and other modern amenities, but we cannot live without water.

Today:

As I've stated, water has already become a major concern in many parts of the world. Therefore, water collection and low pressure spray heads or drip has become the best way to supply irrigation in both agriculture and home landscaping. Both of these trends have shown double-digit growth in recent years despite the ups and downs of our economy. In some parts of the United States, drip is the only type of irrigation system that is allowed for home landscaping.

This is the future of irrigation regardless if we are talking cotton fields or your home landscape. Conserving water is the key to being able to continue our current farming and landscaping habits. Stop in any local diner up in the Panhandle and you will likely find a group of crusty old farmers discussing drip irrigation over coffee. This is their livelihood and they have become experts. Lately I have seen drip/low flow center pivots as close to my hometown as the Vernon/Seymour area. The trend is marching east into higher rainfall country.

The best attribute of drip is that it delivers water slowly. In my country, we refer to a slow steady rain as a "farmer's rain." What the farmers really want is an inch or two of slow rain that will soak in rather than run off. Our fast-moving summer thunderstorms can deliver that amount of rain in fifteen minutes rather than an all-day soaker. Drip is akin to that "farmer's rain" while spray heads and similar devices are like the fast thunderstorm that produces plenty of runoff while very little soaks into the ground.

Water collection will eventually save you money while providing better quality water for your landscape. It is for certain a "no fail" technology where drilling wells or pumping water from remote local sources is generally more expensive and can still fail (it often does in my part of the country where well water is often too salty or laced with other mineral pollution). I strongly recommend folks to start becoming self-sufficient as soon as possible. A few buckets, an old cooler, or any container that will hold water will get you started and you will soon be convinced that installing larger containers or building a holding pond is well worth the effort. The next time your local city or water district enforces outdoor water restrictions you will have a backup plan. Or, even better, if you have enough water storage you may be able to supply all your irrigation needs without having to pay for metered city water at all.

Tomorrow:

We do have a new technology that can make sea water drinkable. Reverse osmosis (RO) of sea water is being used by some of the oil-rich Middle Eastern nations as a solution to supply expanding city populations. They can afford it.

Wichita Falls built an RO unit as a supplement to our fresh water supplies after our last serious drought a decade ago. We have a couple of large reservoirs (Lake Kemp, Lake Diversion) that were built on the Wichita River. The Wichita River is and always has been too salty (saline) for drinking. This RO unit was a comparatively expensive proposition that would only supply an average of ten percent of our daily water needs...but it helped.

These are good examples of how politics usually works. When the general public complains our politicians are obliged to respond. Poor decisions are often made as a result of this kind of pressure. The best long term solution to our local water problem is to build a new reservoir. There is property that we already have rights to build a lake for that exact purpose. Problem is, the new reservoir is way more expensive than these smaller stopgap solutions I've mentioned. No politician wants to have to raise taxes or propose a bond election for any expensive project that will take years to complete. Our budgets are already stretched, so raising extra revenue by any means will likely not help him/her get re-elected...Right?...and so it goes.

One of the easiest ways to conserve water is not using so much treated city water on our lawns and gardens. In most instances, we tend to water on a schedule rather than paying close attention to the weather and rainfall. This is especially true of homeowners that have automatic timers that cause sprinklers to come on. There are rain sensors and underground moisture meters available that can bypass the system. Unfortunately, these cost extra and are not required equipment (yet) so most folks don't have them. Automatic pop-up spray systems are the most wasteful way to irrigate and many homeowners have them now, so most drought contingency plans are aimed specifically at making these people who own such systems obliged to reprogram them according to local ordinance(s). Surcharges and fines for violation are a part of the restrictions.

In the future, water conservation will become second nature. Water recycling and water collection have a bright future for new industry and technology. Water collection for irrigation purposes may well be written into future building codes. Wasting water will be frowned upon by the general public much as smoking in public places is today. Fines and restrictions will escalate as city, state, and possibly federal laws will dictate how public supplies are used and no doubt, as to who will use them. I see this as inevitable. The best way to delay these actions and/or insure public and private rights are protected is to get involved. We need to do this right now, at local levels and state levels. Join and/or form non-profit groups aimed at water conservation.

In the future, most irrigation will be accomplished by drip or something akin to it. Throwing water into the air to run off or evaporate is wasteful. Watering impervious surfaces like concrete will become a code violation. If any form of sprinkler or flood irrigation does survive into the near future, the goal will have to be zero runoff. More likely, above ground spray systems will be restricted to agriculture use only. Cities will employ "water auditors" and likely have a code enforcement department just for water use.

Drilling private water wells may be an option but is not the long term answer. Neither is building more and more reservoirs until every flowing river becomes a chain of lakes. Collecting your own rainwater and turning salt water into fresh water are currently the best options in my opinion. There is only so much fresh water available on this Earth. There is only so much rainfall to replenish resources in any given year. Conservation is the key. Sustainability is the watchword of the 21st Century.

CHAPTER 11
Designing Landscape Garden

Here are some useful facts to consider when designing your landscape:

- When selecting plants, consider function first and foremost. Next, decide on acceptable maintenance levels. Group plants according to irrigation needs whenever possible.

- Always select plants according to how their mature size and appearance fit into your design. Do not select plants based on initial appearance in immature stage of growth.

- Consider adding interest and color to your landscape by rotating annual flowers in small "investment zones" near your house.

- Large growing trees should be planted at least 20 feet from your house. This gives tree roots adequate space to grow and prevents structural damage to your home. Also avoid planting trees closer than five feet from sidewalks and driveways.

Design Dynamics

Paths in a carefully designed sequence, or applied on a larger scale to the movement of people in cars, such as the design of motorway planting for viewing at high speeds.

Unlike architecture, landscape design is concerned with living material, which not only grows changes during the season & over time, but also moves in response to wind or to the touch. Thus the kinetic experience is enriched and made more intimate and varied. The positioning of groups of planting relatives to the path can influence the movement of the observer.

Where a change of direction is desired, ground covers as well as tree & accent shrubs can be used to create pivots point at which one is physically and visually forced to change direction. Pivot points can be extended to form bridging points across paths & roads. If the bridging points are sited close together, these in turn create tension points in the design where the space is narrowed down or constricted before opening up & expanding into another space. Using the idea of line of line of movement, the design can be given a momentum of its own which can be described as a "design speed'. This can be static, slow, moderate or fast; the inherent design force built into any line movement is self-expressive.

Certain misconception exists relating to design line movement. All too often designers seek to create line movement by giving a wavy outline to planting beds. Tree & shrub planting will itself create all the wavy line movement at a higher level as it grows.

Plant material junction should not be too acute. Where the design line movement abuts a building, or two paved areas meets grass areas, the acute point formed results in an awkward space for planting & should be avoided where possible.

Access, Vistas and Arrangement: The point of entry into any given space is always of crucial importance in the design. For instance, one may choose to make it discreet or emphasize it by enframement. A drive or access road into a site may have predominantly vista -like qualities, which can be reinforced with banks of tall & medium shrub & ground cover. Planting flanking each side. The long accepted tradition that when one entered a site, part of the building was first seen & then lost from view, to reemerge later, still remains an effective design technique.

The principle of enframement can be used effectively to draw attention to specifically desirable views & possibly to block out the less desirable elements. For instance massed foreground planting may be used to screen the near view, larger framing plants placing the emphasis on the distant view. Enframement of certain views in connection with doorways or atrium courtyards can best be achieved by the use of large vertical shrubs or small trees with a horizontal branches structure.

Anchoring as a design technique is akin to enframement in so far as it has a similar design purpose, that is to control corners & portion of the design which need reinforcement. The planting of dome-shaped shrubs at the base of small sculptural tree or shrub is another form of anchoring.

CHAPTER 12
Rules of (Green) Thumb for Garden Design

Once you have all your garden measured out, sit down with your graph paper, let one square equal one square foot (adjust this if you have the graph paper with the tiny squares), and start putting this all down on paper. Have the top of the paper be north, and draw a little arrow pointing that way to look more official.

As you do, you will find that you'll need to keep running out to measure more things in the yard in order to make everything line up correctly. You've measured the house and driveway, for example, but wait, how many feet do you have between the driveway and the east corner of the house? So you measure that. Where exactly does the oak tree sit in relation to the fence and the house? So you measure that. The fence and the house are not lining up correctly. So you remeasure that and try to figure out if you transposed a measurement. The oak tree seems to have inadvertently shrunk, though you'd measured it twice. Maybe it's time to take up drinking. Well, okay, but only in moderation.

Of course, that's the way the old timers did it. (Note: I am not old.) These days, you can fix up a nice landscape plan on your phone using an app, or get a more elaborate program for your laptop that will do more than just move a tree symbol around until it looks like it's placed right.

Then it's time for the big step: drawing a plan. Measure your garden. To keep your plan simple, let one-half inch equal one foot. Draw the outline of the garden on your paper.

Protip: Once you have this step finished to your satisfaction, take this paper to the copier and make several copies, and use these as the rough drafts of your garden design.

Now play with that outline. Consider the height and width of these plants. Keep short plants in front and tall plants in back, and use those pictures you've clipped (whether out of a magazine or found on the internet) to make sure the colors match. Do you want soft colors, such as purple catmint, pink petunias, and silver Artemisia? Or do you want a fiesta of red salvia and "Yellow Boy" marigolds?

Also, consider when your perennials bloom. You may love purple asters and pink sea thrift, but that color pairing won't be happening, because the asters bloom in fall and the sea thrift blooms in spring.

It's a good idea to put the tall plants in back and short plants in front. Green side up. Match the plants to the amount of sun that's available. Set your shade plants near the trees, while the full sun plants will need to be right out in the sun.

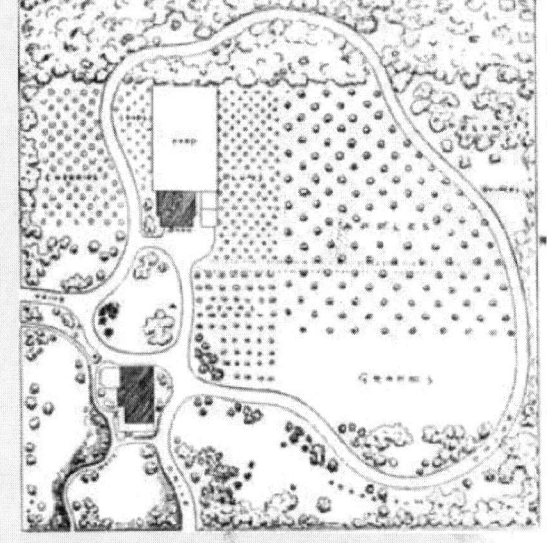

As you draw your plan, generally a good rule of thumb is to arrange them by height – tallest plants in back, shortest ones in the back. Or, as with an island bed, tallest plants in the middle, going to the shortest on the edges. But you can also blend several different varieties of plants that are the same size, the same way as you would blend several different flowers in a flower arrangement, for a good blend of colors and shapes. And you don't have to be exact on regimenting sizes. A garden isn't a lineup of soldiers on dress parade, after all.

You can arrange the plants in any way. You can arrange them in a parterre, a formal setting with neat rows, tidy edged shrubs. Or you can have a wild, natural garden with plants arranged as if they were growing wild. Chances are you will be someplace between these two extremes in your own garden.

Also, to make more of an impact, plant your perennials in drifts of 3, 5, or 7. These groups provide more of an impact than just planting one of every plant (unless you have a specimen plant that's as big as an elephant).

Protip: It's a good idea to have a little out-of-the-way place in your garden where you keep extra plants – those you've picked up when on sale but can't find a place for, plants you've picked up out of curiosity, plants you've gotten from friends and neighbors that don't quite fit into your gardening plan, or things you need to find a proper place for but haven't gotten to yet.

This little garden can get helpful, though. If you have a plant in your regular garden that suddenly croaks, you can grab a full-grown specimen from your little side garden and pop it into your regular garden, if you're so inclined, thereby filling the gap.

You can also keep your cutting garden here, so you can just pop out the back door and cut a few flowers for bouquets inside the house. Then you won't have to swipe flowers from your front gardens and leave holes in it.

CHAPTER 13
Design with Family in Mind

Here are a few pointers which will help the process, of course some will apply to you and some won't, depending upon the type and size of your family.

From babies through to teenagers, your garden will evolve and change as much as they will. If you intend on having a family play in your own back yard then designing your garden landscape keeping your family in mind can be somewhat of a challenge, but certainly easier than you might think.

The most important aspect of a landscape and garden design when you are catering for family and especially young children, is their safety.

Safety is paramount and should be considered not only for the grounds but also for the equipment and toys they will be playing with outside.

Open space is by far the most appropriate but it can be a little boring, so it's really a matter of striking a balance between your garden desires and the play area.

If your children are still small, then you are able to achieve this quite easily, usually they are quite content to stay in a relatively small play area with toys that will keep them occupied and it's probable, that when they are outside, you or someone else is outside too watching over them.

However when they become a little more independent, it's then that the design of your garden will need to have a few more changes made to it.

Young children, at first anyway, don't understand the boundaries from a garden edge and will often run straight onto the flower bed to get their ball or some other stray toy, so my advice is your edging has to be well defined and easily seen, this will speed up the learning curve for them.

Your gardens need to have sturdy shrubs and flowering bushes rather than the delicate bulbs, perennials and annuals. These more delicate plants can easily be destroyed even from little feet.

Your choice of plants have to be children friendly and by that I mean avoid plants that could cause irritations to the skin, or produce berries that are poisonous or nuts that fall onto the ground that they can eat or will hurt their feet when walked on etc.

Tools are another aspect to the safety and design of your garden, have a tool shed or an area somewhere in your design that is inaccessible to children. Poisons and Fertilizers need to be kept out of reach as well as all your tools.

Always try to design the landscape, where possible, to have a visual of the area where they will be playing from the part of the house that you spend the most time in, like the family orientated rooms.

If you are able to take a quick glance out the window or door and see them, makes it safer than if they were totally out of site, hence the larger open spaces in your yard, the less private areas you have in your garden design, the less chance there will be of them hurting themselves and you not knowing about it.

Staying in sight is still very important, even though this age group are a lot more confident in their own ability this can also work against them and accidents can still happen in the garden. Because of this it is important to keep the play area clear from tools and trip hazards like hoses left unreeled, rakes and shovels left out etc.

Trampolines are also very popular and although the designs of this equipment have improved with full cages etc. there is still a lot of the older styles in service. Try to keep these out in the open, plenty of space around them so if there is a fall off then it minimizes the injury. One idea is to consider mulching around the base area to soften any fall. If you are just placing it on the lawn, you might want to move it around regularly so it will not shade the grass too much.

Storage areas have to be considered for the kids push bikes, if kids have an area to place their bikes when not in use, it will keep your garden safer.

It's probably more important and only if possible of course to try and avoid too many steps in your garden when catering for these kids, they like to run around a lot so ramping and clear areas are ideal. This isn't always possible depending on the type of house block you have but for those that able, you'll find it much safer for all the kids concerned.

Now as far as plants go…well you should probably stay with flowering shrubs although selected pocket areas, that are out of contact with the bigger play areas, are usually safe to have.

Even garden boxes or border gardens around the entertaining area filled with bulbs, Annuals and Perennials and delicate shrubs like Fuchsias etc. can be quite successful and will provide a lot of fragrance and color, for those times you are out there with friends.

CHAPTER 14
Containers Bed Borders for Plants Ideas

For late summer containers stealing the show, make foliage focal point. This easy-care planter uses, at the end of the season, vibrant "orange rustic" scales (Solenostemon scutellarioides), which are identified by their rusty leaves that last until the first frost. The filler in this space-saving pot is "taps" (Impaticens sp.) That contain small mandarin blossoms and glossy dark leaves that contrast nicely with the scales of bronze. Finally, the "yellow moon" (Torenia sp.)

Made for shade

A simple follow-up formula is all you need to create a drama in a container. Here, it takes only four stops to transfer the illusion of a floor-length gown. The key to pulling this piece starts from the raised planter so that the vibrant 'Celebration' and 'Florida Sweetie' pop up eye-level. Clusters of white collarbone flower fill the empty spaces between the legs of cadium and the actual container also disappears, which means you can use any stand-alone container. The last attention grabber is graceful crawling Jenny Spilling on both sides. Put this planter in the shade and water regularly for a great, easy-to-maintain view.

A traditional tabletop container

If you need evidence that a regular and simple farmer has the potential to brighten what would be a side table filled with the backyard then look here. This copper bulb, instead of its competitor, complements the zinc alloys. Yellow calibrachoas - which look a little like petunias - appear on the edge of the container. Then, the hidden spots of purple verbenas create another unexpected but powerful focal point in this outdoor garden conversation space. If you want your farmer to have this beautiful sense of flow, be sure to specify the "plus" calibrachoa for this container as it grows less than the mounding version.

Free standing modern container

The planter at the faux-lead end is a timeless choice, but the cylindrical shape of these long fiberglass jars gives it a clean and modern engineering feel. This type of design can work well in any decor as it focuses on familiar shapes. Choosing a neutral tone or texture for your containers highlights the unique natural beauty of the color of flowers and foliage. Here, the pearl chain creates a lot of architectural drama through its unique shape, while calibrachoa purple and blue agertatum add the right dose of brightness to add depth to this subtle arrangement.

Modern hanging container

Hanging containers are a simple way to bring gardens into limited spaces, or to add beauty to your space in simple, unexpected ways. For this unique design, it gives a mixture of structural juices a bold internal structure, and takes center stage on a fiberglass planter. Purple flower fan permeates lush greenery. Fan flower is unique because all of its flowers have their chip on one side. In southern Equatoria, these plants can be evergreen. Given its bold and bright color, it offers a refreshing contrast to the deep, dark container hanging in the air.

Modern tabletop container

This exquisitely organic look comes from contrasting the strong and elegant lines of a modern container with the soft breeze movement of natural plants. A carefully selected group of beautiful containers embody rich and warm metallic tones in this well-designed outdoor oasis. The handsome farmer on the surface of the earth has a glaze-like shape and mixes different juices with the pink columns of 'ptilotus', a bottle factory that is home to Australia. The broad-leaved Kalanthus scraps and the dwarf golden arborvitaes form the basis of this masterpiece, which can decorate this suit just as easily as it can highlight the center of the dining table in the backyard.

Rectangular containers

This durable galvanized metal filling - the jewel of the flea market - is filled with scandalous beauty with a creamy blend of lantanas and impatiens. This dense container with a Joseph Maroon coat, Green Collie and Genie Yellow Creeper is designed to highlight the back porch, or to greet guests with a sense of joy and happiness on the front porch easily. Coleus varieties were first introduced to Europe in the eighteenth century, and their popularity remains high today. Due to its tropical history, it's not too cold, so don't plan to make it a part of this container too early in the spring.

Rustic hanging container

The most important key to this rural aesthetic is ensuring that the container is not overlapping. You are sure to love the look of this arrangement when you give flowers to breathe. This rusty metal bucket, which was found, is another unpopular market in the flea market, studded with miserable balls, abundant pigeon flowers, coleus, and other sweets. But what is not crowded, which can prevent plants from getting enough light. To get more rustic charm inspired by the south, try hanging this arrangement on a branch. This will add to the easy casual feeling.

Rural tabletop containers

The simple galvanized metal tool box is an unexpected container for gardening containers that fits the whole natural spring setting. Here, it showcases a classic arrangement of bright green mint, red geranium, and sweet white yellow, for a light and fresh container. You will also love how easy it can move this around the park thanks to the built-in handle. However, what she loves most is the rustic charm of the checkered metal that contrasts with the soft and subtle colors of flowers. This is a beautiful study of the soft and hard elements in the container garden design.

Romantic free container

Relax and visualize this traditional metal jar in a dreamy garden or on a light-covered balcony filled with light. The jar itself is designed with classic Victorian lines, giving it a romantic element, but the arrangement makes it a fascinating reality. The key to designing this look is to combine contrasting textures. Here, the grassy cordyline, the sweet pink dyanthos, sweep the sweet potato vine of "ace of spades", bright blue lobelia, and Angelonia's pink constellations, in a succession of bright colors and loud celebrations. Designed in a beautiful shape, but a simple monochromatic tone, from the vase, this creates a stop container for your garden.

Romantic hanging container

This romantic container garden captures feelings of magic and mystery through bright colors and a beautiful feeling of movement. To achieve these effects, you will need to try to change the range of flowers and greenery to produce a unstable unruly feeling, "growing in a garden" that keeps this basket relaxed. Starting with choosing a hanging basket of moss-made metal, Dianth's elder is mixed with younger petunias, while various English tears and baby tears dangle on both sides. The effect is the feeling of beauty in flowering, bursting in wonder from this colorful basket.

Romantic tabletop container

Laying layering is an integral part of assembling this amazing container. Although the handcrafted bowl that forms the central part of this impressive arrangement may look delicate, it is made of recycled concrete materials. Its wide shape accommodates many of the same flowers and plants used in other "romantic containers", only to display more exotic containers similar to the flowering arrangement of flowers. If you select flowers like dianthus, then this romantic Tabletop container will start with the right colors, tones and shapes. Its effect will be absolutely elegant and beautiful. Sit on the table for an evening drink, or casual chat, and let romance bloom.

Romantic wall swag container

This rich and vibrant design puts flowers in the spotlight. This will literally and figuratively sense a beautiful view. The elegant container floats above a decorated brick wall, and is covered with enlarged flowers, which include floral petunias, very tender baby tears, and round clusters of pink dyanthes. For this arrangement, the focus is entirely on flowers. In fact, the hidden pot is just here to provide grounding support. Depending on your design, you may want to consider a series of these containers as a way to highlight the garden wall, add color and focus on something you've always wanted to ignore. You will not have to imagine beauty - it will be right in front of you.

Bring on the sun

Here it comes - a beautiful container in the sun, that is. This high-maintenance, exciting health-care container features "diffuse miniature salmon soap", but leaves room for fustail asparagus ferns and a 6-inch bowl of potos 'Neon'. Everything is placed in a glazed ceramic container, with a bright green color that complements the natural colors of the farmer. This is a beautiful example to preserve the aesthetic of a simple container garden. They called SunPatiens - a cross-breed strain between the New Guinea hybrid and wild species - the central and bright focus of this arrangement. Then, let everything else help them simply shine.

Show your true colors

Everyone in the south realizes that college sports are fun family fun, and what is the best way to show and share your team spirit instead of bringing your favorite colors to your container garden? This beautiful design brings the Bengal tigers - plants in this LSU themed container thriving in a moist and sun-mix mixture part. You'll find a bunch of shades of purple from bright, bold to subtle and subtle, all in a festive container. You can take this idea and replace the colors of your favorite team for the seasonal celebration that combines nature and culture - and what could be better?

Summer taste!

Let's hear it for the elephant's ear! Its huge leaves - the secret of this lavish combination - create large-scale drama. It allows you to fill in the blanks with small colored flowers. This arrangement is placed in a concrete jar with total texture to give it a dried finish. You will love how the delicate flowers decorate the same jar feel. One of the beautiful wonders of an elephant's ear is that it blooms first and then fruits. The fruit was described as making the stem look like corn on the piece. Whatever you think, looks gorgeous in your summer container.

CHAPTER 15
Designing with Evergreens

Evergreens keep their foliage throughout the entire year and provide lasting structure throughout the landscape, no matter what the season. They can be used for a variety of functions, including that of foundation plantings, specimen items or screening. The underlying principle of design is to combine the perfect number of evergreens, deciduous flowering or non-flowering shrubs, perennials and annuals to create an attractive landscape that also serves a purpose.

When designing, the first step is to plan the foundation. Foundation plants are those used to anchor the main structure of the house. They also serve the purpose of making a home more energy efficient by blocking cold winds and creating an insulating effect. For this reason, I mostly use evergreens along foundations, because they supply continuous structure, texture, color and screening. Some of the more popular evergreens used for foundation plantings include boxwood, compact holly, cherry laurel and some varieties of euonymus. Consider how tall and wide the plants you choose will be at their mature size, as to avoid future overcrowding, and allow enough bed size for planting room. It is important as well to be aware of any windows and doors that could potentially be blocked from view. The use of plants that are somewhat compact is recommended.

For a single accent in the landscape, specimen plantings are used. Specimen plants are usually of a unique nature and are used to make a statement or create impact. Some of the specimen evergreens I use in my designs include:

- Weeping Blue Atlas Cedar,
- Weeping Norway Spruce,
- Blue Globe Spruce,
- Weeping White Pine,
- Hinoki Cypress,
- Dwarf White Pine,
- Dwarf Mugo Pine,
- Golden Oriental Spruce
- Dwarf Cryptomeria.

Examples of Foundation Evergreens:

Boxwood is an excellent evergreen for foundation plantings due to its relatively slow growth pattern and rounded shape. Compact forms of Boxwood that I frequently use in foundation designs include the cultivars 'Green Mound', 'Green Gem', 'Wintergem', 'Green Velvet' and 'Variegata'. Boxwood 'Wintergem', 'Green Gem' and 'Green Velvet' are all hardy in USDA zones 4-9, while 'Green Mound' is hardy in zones 5-8 and 'Variegata' to zones 5-9. 'Green Mound' and 'Green Gem' Boxwood grow to a height of 2-3 feet high by wide. 'Wintergem' grows 2-4 feet in height by 3-5 feet in width, while 'Variegata' and 'Green Velvet' reach a taller stature of 3-5 feet in height by 3-4 feet in width. Foliage on the mentioned varieties of boxwood is green, except that of Boxwood 'Variegata', which displays green and creamy white variegated foliage. Boxwood can be easily maintained with pruning once or twice a season to keep its rounded shape.

Hollies for foundation plantings come in a variety of forms. The two I most often use are Ilex 'Compacta' (Compact Holly) and Ilex 'Hoogerdorn' (Hoogerdorn Holly), both hardy in USDA zones 6-9. 'Ilex Compacta' displays a lighter green foliage on a 4-6 tall by wide plant, while Ilex 'Hoogerdorn' has relatively darker foliage with lighter tips and matures to a more compact plant of 2 feet tall by 4 feet wide. There are a couple of other hollies that are useful in foundation plantings for adding height or to break up a row of smaller foundation plantings, as between windows or at the end of a bed. 'Dragon Lady' Holly, perfect for the end of a foundation planting as a single piece, is a slow growing dark leaved holly that stays narrow at 4-6 feet wide and grows to a height of 10-20 feet. 'Steeds Holly' grows only 6-8 feet tall by 5-6 feet wide and is a good candidate. Holly and boxwood each prefer to be grown in full sun to partial shade with moderate watering.

For larger spaces, Chery Laurel 'Otto Luyken' (Prunus laurocerasus 'Otto Luyken') is a dark green broad-leaved evergreen hardy to USDA zones 6-8. It grows to a height of 3-4 feet tall by 6-8 feet wide, making it a good candidate for hiding unsightly cement foundations. It has a moderate to fast growth rate and will thrive in a range of conditions, including full sun to full shade. Tiny, creamy white flowers in upright clusters produced in early spring make a great contrast to the plant's darker foliage. Prunus laurocerasus 'Otto Luyken' prefers moderate watering and a well-drained soil.

For variegated foliage, members of the Euonymus family, including Euonymus 'Silver King' and 'Gold Spot' will bring some nice interest to your foundation planting. Euonymus 'Silver King' is a moderate grower with a narrow habit, reaching a mature height of 5-8 feet tall by 2-3 feet wide. It can be maintained at a smaller size and makes a colorful addition as a backdrop in a foundation planting with its green and white variegated foliage. Euonymus 'Gold Spot', displaying green leaves with yellow variegation, can reach a mature height of 5-10 feet and width of 3-6 feet wide, but can also be easily maintained at a desired stature with pruning once or twice a year. Both cultivars are hardy in USDA zones 6-9 and require moderate watering.

The foundation plantings described here are those which are most desired by designers and homeowners for both their attributes and hardiness. The next step in design is to explore some of the specimen plantings that are available to enhance your landscape even further.

CONCLUSION

You will need to maintain your landscape garden the same way you would do so for an in-the-ground garden. You just must do so on a smaller scale. The drawback of planting in pots is that they will have lesser amounts of nutrients in the soil. They will also hold less water compared to garden beds. Because of this, you must make sure you maintain the water and nutrient levels in the soil. You will need to this on a regular basis. This will help the plants survive and grow healthy flowers and leaves. It will also make sure the plants produce edible vegetables. You should be aware of a few things you need to do to maintain your garden. This includes feeding the soil, avoiding soil compaction, and pruning or caging.

.I recommend using organic methods, just as when you prepared the soil. To do this, you will need manure or compost and a small garden fork. When the soil in the pot is moist, break up the upper layer (four to six inches) with the garden fork. Then, till (or mix) the compost or manure into this layer, again with the garden fork. When you are done, spread more on top of the soil. Then water the plant well.

You can also use store-bought plant feed. Garden centers have organic plant food for sale. You should try to use these if you can. Most of these kinds of feed should be mixed with water before you apply them. Then, when you water your plants, you are also feeding them.

Just like in a garden bed, it is important to prevent the soil in your pots from being compacted. One way this happens is by leaning your weight on the soil when you are gardening. This is more common in garden beds. Gardeners will kneel or walk on their beds, which crushes the soil underfoot. But it can happen in large planters as well. Be careful not to compact the soil in this way.

A more common way soil is compacted in pots is by watering. If you do not use a watering can that has a rose to break up the water, or if you do not use a nozzle on your hose that makes a fine mist, you risk pounding the soil into a hard crust. Of course, the best way to prevent this is by using the proper tools.

But if you do not have these kinds of tools, there is another solution. You can place a broken pot or plate in the soil. Then, let the water flow onto the hard surface. This will lessen the force of the water before it touches the soil.

Before you water your plants, you should also break up the soil. You can do this with a fork or a trowel. Doing this will allow water and air to pass more easily to the roots.

Many of your plants should not be left to grow however they want. You will have to control their growth with stakes, cages, or pruning.

Pruning makes sure plants do not grow out of control. It also promotes the kind of growth you want. For example, you should prune tomato plants. You will want to pinch the stems that grow at 45-degree angles from the main stem. Leave the stems that grow at right angles to the main stem. The 45-degree stems take nutrients away from any tomatoes growing on that stem. Leaving them on will result in many tomatoes not becoming ripe. Talk to a master gardener about what kinds of pruning the other veggies in your garden need.

Harvesting time varies with each crop. For you to understand the ideal time to harvest and the best means of picking to avoid damaging. The followings are a few things you need to know:

Check the seed packs to understand the harvest time better. Check the number of days to maturity. If you are a new gardener, keep a record in a journal to help you make notes on your observations. Record what you have planted and the date to know the time they would be ready for harvesting. It will help a lot pending when you familiarized yourself with each variety.

As a gardener, you will learn gradually to be patient and not harvest before crops are ready. For example, pumpkins might look big enough to pick and eat, but they are not good to reap until the stem dries off, turned hard and vines die out. If you pick them earlier, the seeds might not be adequately matured to keep. The taste as well would not be at its best. Cut the stalks at about 5cm from the fruit to increase storage time. Let the pumpkins dry-off in the sun for one or two days to make their skin tough. They have a long storage life if they are well stored.

Another example is beans. They can be picked while they are young or give them more days to be matured before harvesting so that you can get the best nutritional value out of them

The maturity times of beans varied with the variety you grow. Variety like runner beans is as short as six weeks and could keep producing for about four months. Variety like bush beans and climbing start producing at about nine weeks provide you with abundant harvest for about three months. Zucchinis are ideally harvested young (approximately 10cm long if they are to be pickled) since they grow faster in hot weather and could suddenly turn into a marrow.

Plants use a vast amount of their energy in fruiting and flowering. Thus, it is significant to ensure they acquire enough soil nutrients to assist them to produce plenty of crops, and also to build their immune system, making them more resistance to diseases and pests.

Bear in mind when harvesting crops like leafy greens, the best time to harvest them are late afternoon or early evening instead of morning to prevent eating avoidable nitrates in your food. The sunlight must have converted the nitrates in the daytime. Plants will discharge or share about thirty percent of the energy produced using photosynthesis in the day with the root area. This assists in feeding beneficial microbes that helpful to plant directly. While the microorganisms in turn discharge nutrients to the plants to keep growing.

Printed in Great Britain
by Amazon